ELIZABETH JANE PARKER

COSMIC ENTRANCEMENT & THE BIG SEE

Also by Elizabeth Jane Parker

The Theory and Revelation of Angels Cosmos Earth A.C.E.
Grosvenor House, 2009
ISBN 978-1907211812

Voices from Heaven
AuthorHouse 2011
ISBN 978-1456771782

The Mirror of Actuality: God is indeed personal
to every single person upon the Earth
Memoirs Publishing 2012
ISBN 978-1909020443

ELIZABETH JANE PARKER

COSMIC ENTRANCEMENT & THE BIG SEE

MEMOIRS
Cirencester

Published by Memoirs

MEMOIRS
PUBLISHING

25 Market Place, Cirencester, Gloucestershire, GL7 2NX
info@memoirsbooks.co.uk www.memoirspublishing.com

Cosmic Entrancement & The Big SEE

No part of this book may be reproduced or transmitted in any form or by any means, graphic, electronic, or mechanical, including photocopying, recording, taping or by any information storage or retrieval system, without the permission in writing from the copyright holder.

The right of Elizabeth Jane Parker to be identified as the author of this work has been asserted in accordance with the Copyright, Designs and Patents Act 1988 sections 77 and 78.

The views expressed in this work are solely those of the author and do not necessarily reflect the views of the publisher, and the publisher hereby disclaims any responsibility for them.

ISBN: 978-1-86151-051-8

This Book is dedicated to
Our Lord of Love and Compassion

On the 28th June 2013 I met outside a well-known supermarket a man in a wheelchair collecting for *Motor Neurone Disease*. My feelings were one of admiration, not pity for this man who was both a hero and prisoner of his biology. This man was asking for funding and hope for a cure of this debilitating condition to his health. I gave him some money. However; Yashua Jesus Christ would have healed him with love, honour and truth with powers of the Universe and through his ownership with God. I felt powerless and saddened that we have all misunderstood his blessings to us within our modern age.

Many people walked past him and looked embarrassed at his wasting figure sitting quietly with his collection box; it seemed to reduce his appeal to one of begging within a modern world of materialism and fast living. This disadvantaged man was subjected again to the power of money which buys research and healthcare and yet we all have the ability to give what we can for each other and to heed the lessons that money cannot truly buy us health and happiness. I felt love and friendship towards this man who was cheerful and communicative with thanks for my donation.

Love is the greatest power for us all to own and from this we give to our brethren and sisters of life with the grace of God, knowing that a man called Jesus, a man of greatness and kindness, walked our Earth so many years ago with his powers of love, compassion and teaching for us all to know the truth about God and his divine love of us all. Through my own life I have learnt about the power of love and the war against evil which seeks to dominate us all. From this I have learnt that Jesus died for us to recognize this and absolve all things with forgiveness and compassion, He has taught me this and through our modern age so we all can learn the most simple aspects of love and compassion from our **Lord of the Heavens.**

Elizabeth P.

Table of Contents

About this book
The Efficacious Education
Epigraph: The Intellectual Emphasis on Truth
Epigraph: For there is Hope

INTRODUCTION
Poem: Beautiful Bath and Malmesbury

CHAPTER ONE:
The Connection and Vibration of Truth
Lesson

CHAPTER TWO:
Hark! The Herald Angels Sing
Poem: The Inspiration of Cambridgeshire

CHAPTER THREE:
The Fruits of Wisdom
Wisdom Personified
Wisdom from Above
Poem: The Winding Steps

CHAPTER FOUR:
The Lord of Truth

CHAPTER FIVE:
The Sanctification of Virtue
Poem: Aspirations
Sanctification & Virtue

CHAPTER SIX:
Divine Divinity

CHAPTER SEVEN:
Cosmic Entrancement
In the Beginning
The Beauty of Life
Poem: Christchurch 2013
The Theorem

CHAPTER EIGHT:
Intuitive Intuition
A Poem for All Seasons
The Revelatory Spin of Sight
Poem: A Bournemouth Story

CHAPTER NINE:
Fortitude and Ambivalences
The Divine Providence

AFTERWORD:
One God, One Truth, One Love
The Beginning: The Cosmic Entrancement & the Big SEE

About this Book
Elizabeth Jane Parker

THIS BOOK has been brought about by inspiration and the love of life. The teachings of God and Jesus Christ have long been ignored and misunderstood by fellowship. We are all upon a primeval agenda through life and understanding. The foresight of our responsibility upon this planet has now moved into somatic solipsism with life and reasoning. We forget as humanity the reasoning and intelligence we all have. We simply overlook the reality and reasoning of life on Earth. Somatic individualism becomes important and unification of our spirit and soul become one of denial about our future upon a planet of limitation.

The summing up of our lives is that we share this planet. We share knowledge. We share proceeds of our universal knowledge and create our lives of being together; much easier with a simple truth. The villain of us all is explained in one word; *desire*. This word encompasses many meanings against the wisdom of God and his eternal love for us all.

The proof we all have is our body of miracle. We live, we breathe, we learn, we grow, we understand, we cherish, we love. The attributes of our lives is to know that God is real and that from his teachings through Jesus Christ we can find a better way of living, sharing and knowing the truth and the facts of reality. Many people decide that to live a life without belief is a better option and through their disbelief they attempt to disprove God's reasoning. However, God is ever present watching us all and waiting.

Our learning is but a simple truth. That truth is about love and honour superseding the influences of opinion, judgement and procrastination. Our souls are united in Heaven and we do know about reasoning and that reasoning is the knowledge we accumulate once we understand the precision of God and his love for us all. To believe in love is the greatest asset we can all own within this materialistic world of desire.

Do we listen? To listen and to see objectively is the wisdom uniting with compassion and understanding the beauty and fascination of nature and ourselves. We are nature as humanity and we are apt to forget that we too are made from nature. How did this nature occur? How did we evolve into a modern day dilemma? Our world is still fragmented. Great divides occur with opinion, judgement and procrastination. We as one in Heaven have lost our way as humanity and unification on Earth and the wonders of life itself. How do we find God amongst the unenlightened modernism and materialism? How do we find him and love him unconditionally, returning his devotion to us all?

To find God is to know that he is there waiting for us all with open arms, but before we find him we journey through life and reasoning. We journey with Earth and her gifts. We journey with learning and living with God's creation and life. We learn about the wonders of life and the Universe. We learn about ourselves living within limitations. We learn about the gifts we all have. We learn by life itself and the beauty of nature and the gifts of life we receive. So we appreciate, learn and observe using our intelligence throughout the globe and the learning sphere named *Earth*.

The story of humanity is about living a life with memories. Each day, each second we move forward with Earth as our Mother of existence. We move forward learning, understanding and proactively listening to the vibrations we all have. Each day we change for a future that awaits us all. The prosperity of us is to carry the treasures of knowledge forward with virtue. To understand that darkness can become a polymorphous affinity with virtue through our lessons and we can disperse all misgivings and doubts with love, honour and truth as our guide through life. *And did those feet* so many years ago come with love and honour to reach our hearts with *Holy Spirit* for us all to seek with the comforting assurance that the door is always open should we so wish to know and learn from God's Holy Ordinance. The Cosmic Entrancement is our passage and understanding with life and reasoning and from this we learn about life. We learn about the challenges that beset us all within a world of diversity and change. We learn about our truth with individualism but also the outer sanctum with virtue and truth.

And hereby we know that we are of the truth, and shall assure our hearts before him. For if our heart condemn us, God is greater than our heart, and knoweth all things.

John 3 : 19-20

The Efficacious Education

THE SYSTEMATIC *workings of divination*, healing and the holy word are not necessarily one of ordination with orthodox and influence but one of belief in all virtuous understanding. The triumph of raising individual vibration and metaphysics can be controversially sought without meditation utilizing transcendence as an escape velocity from traumatic concepts and attribute with learning, wisdom and timescale. The escape mechanisms for life and modern stress will accumulate no matter how we meditate and levitate our existence with Earth and her vibrations. So, from all aspects of society and dilemma the understanding we achieve with God is to know this Earth and her projection of life is the systematic monopoly using our light as spiritual alignment against misaligned people and malfunction with love, honour and forgiveness. Thus, meditation is purely personal and through choice with *Holy Ordinance*. The aspects of life will always emerge again no matter how or what we perceive as personalisation and globalisation with spiritual containment. The power of prayer and love is the realistic aspect of life upon Earth and the *Angels of Harmony* seek to blend our lives with heavenly vibration through acknowledging, appreciation and love for humanity as a whole. For we all belong together upon this Planet of life.

The truth and realistic discernment with life has a natural law of physics and divinity as one. The provocation of

Earthly challenge is one of spectrum and idealism with material and matter formulating into a factual pathway through transition and evolution. There is no easy way of explanation for a generation in denial; however, to bring the *velocity vibrations of God* is to move ever forward with our Earth and her contribution to all of life. The overriding factor with God is simply the virtuous aspect of learning and intent. In our world today many people actually fail to see themselves as a living miracle within the realms of spirituality, intelligence and science. From this perspective we can eventually begin to understand all divine procedures with angelic ordination and the SEE of reality both spiritually and biologically.

The minefield of fundamentalism brings many people to confuse the teachings of Christ with that of *Established Monism*. This brings many to misunderstand about the Holy Word of God and his Son Yashua Jesus Christ. The guidelines and introspection of us as individuals is to seek through life and find our light through the darkness and hypothesis of life's journey with virtuous intention and love. It is that simple with analogy and supposition, but the reality in practice is the test to our virtue and reality with God. Seeking with our soul and eternally learning from life and transition is a path of reasoning realistic dimensions through time and space. The Cosmic Entrancement constitutes the fundamental aspects of life and learning with Heaven and Earth as one. Thus our soul endeavours to project God and his divinity with time and eternity.

Jesus Yashua Christ was a redeemer through teaching God's

word with compassion and simplicity for all to understand. His word was about the seven sacraments of virtue and the path of understanding our Creator. Our Lord of virtue had compassion to all of humanity whatever creed they may choose was the Christlight of fellowship and honour. Our Lord brought his teachings to thousands and through his miracles and love for us all gave his life when fundamentalists of his time persecuted his light. For our Lord taught us all to live, learn and understand the messages and love of our heavenly father. His cup was empty each day he lived and through this lesson he taught us all about learning and living with God our Father. He taught us about God's love for us living within a dark world and journeying with evil. And thus, through his lessons we learnt to understand forgiveness and love for all those who dishonour us through life.

To summarize, his divinity was one of passion and involvement with life and meaning. His contribution as a prophet was to seek out all those people who were in pain and turmoil attempting to understand this world and the next. His love and honour to us all was truly heard by many, as well as his philanthropic teaching of *Holy Scripture and the Universal Law* with virtue and true love. He is and was our salvation in a world of dilemma and downfall. Through this work we understand bible study and the stories related bring about a new interpretation for people to choose to believe within our ordinary but miraculous lives upon Earth.

And Jesus said "Man shall not live by bread alone, but every word that proceedeth out of the mouth of God."

The intellectual emphasis upon truth is the realities of spirituality with growth. To live everyday with biology and Earth's vibration is to know the keys of Heaven allow our soul and spirit to understand God's Blessings. His love is the eternal diameter of understanding all aspects of virtue and love. Upon our planet Earth we walk softly with God, knowing and living his beauty, love and monism with creation.

Elizabeth Jane Parker 2012.

For there is hope of a tree, if it be cut down, that IT WILL SPROUT AGAIN, and that the tender branch thereof will not cease. Though the root thereof wax old in the Earth, and the stock thereof die in the ground; yet through the scent of water it will bud, and bring forth boughs like a plant.

Job 14 : 7-9

Introduction

"United we stand, divided we fall."

Robert Grosseteste Medieval Bishop of Lincoln and Leicester

Born 1175 A.D

THE HOLY BIBLE, how do we as individuals understand the resonance and healing divination of the word? From our belief and teachings in a realistic world, we are all walking through an endless maze with life and reasoning. In order to understand and truly obey our virtuous intentions we are often as humanity met with dishonour from our brethren. And turning *the other cheek* becomes a reaction against the dishonour.

The truth and realities of life are bestowed by the virtues and truth of understanding our passage through life. The many contradictions blocking our way can be imperturbably impervious with the simplicity of wisdom and truth lighting our way through the darkness.

Now therefore hearken unto me, O ye children:
For blessed are those who keep my ways.
Hear instruction, and be wise,
And refuse it not.
Blessed is the man that hears me,
Watching daily at my gates,
Waiting at the posts of my doors
For whoso finds me finds life,
And shall obtain favour of the LORD
But he who sins against me wrongs his own soul

Proverbs 8 : 32-36

What do we learn from the above passage from the Holy Bible? What does it mean to the ordinary man in the street? The average and accessible information of today is one of technological advancement and science with fact. However, this message was written with a deep meaning of life and reasoning. Many people are subjected to their own fears and the fragility of life and passage. Understanding and caring for our soul is something we all overlook as a reality. So, teaching all aspects of virtue and learning simplicity of fundamental reasoning and wisdom becomes one of identification with inner sanctum and outer sanctum containing and projecting the beauty of life, but understanding the impermanence of existence with biological functioning. So upon the road of salvation we cherish the challenge and love our soul with kindness, fortitude and forgiveness against all others who dishonour us. We learn to challenge with kindness, without anger, and we learn most of all to move forward upon our journey every day with Earth and her electrodynamics of change. Our soul is the eternal monochromatic veneration with God and the true colours and vibration with Earth and the Universe.

> *My soul, wait only upon God;*
> *For my expectation is from him.*
> *He is my rock and my salvation:*
> *He is my defence: I shall not be moved.*
> *In God is my salvation and my glory:*
> *The rock of my strength and my refuge, is in God.*
>
> **The Holy Bible**
> *(Psalm 62 : 5 -7)*

Spiritual revelation is a minor part of our actual *escape velocity* from the traumas of life and resonance. We all move daily with our biology and spiritual aspects with perceptions and our life is determined by choice within the free world. From this balance we understand from our individual life that we all belong to God through virtue. The sins of life are many and people without belief often *flounder* with virtuous intent through misconception about outer and inner sanctum. Further education is always available with *Elemental Scholastics* within life. However, the systematic workings of self-containment bring all conceptions with virtue, understanding the realities of life, reasoning and above all true love. So, true love is about virtue, containment and moving each day with our Earth and her gifts to us all.

The aerodynamics of energy perpetuating physics and photosynthesis of life giving properties is realism with spiritual containment and appreciation of a miracle living, breathing and understanding of life with personality and nirvana as truth; for nirvana and perfect harmony await us all in the future of heaven and earth together working and understanding the miracle of evolution, life and journey around the sun. For as with the Buddha teachings, he says, *"life is the journey, not the destination"* — but to see ourselves through physical chemistry is part of this journey with learning, understanding and procreating virtue no matter what.

"We search and wonder within the confines of life and reasoning and through this gift we all learn about our identity through life and the character of incarnation and life together."

> *Wisdom has built her house,*
> *She has hewn out her seven pillars:*
> *She has killed the beasts: she has mingled her wine;*
> *She has sent forth her maidens, she cried upon the highest places of the city*
> *Whoso is simple, let him turn hither:*
> *As for him that wants understanding she says to him*
> *Come, eat my bread,*
> *And drink the wine which I have mingled*
> *Forsake the foolish and live;*
> *And go the way of understanding.*
>
> *Proverbs 9 : 1-6*

The seven pillars of virtue represent our *Chakras and elemental revelation* with Earth. The realities of our lives as a journey are about our choices and wisdom. For healing our lives is essential for our journey and vibration with the *Wonders of the Universe* and eternity connecting with all sources of reasoning our intelligence with wisdom and the realities of life itself. Life is indeed the journey and the revelation of time unfolding. Through unfolding we as humanity need guidance from pure aspects of *Heavenly Virtue* and this is one of the teachings of Christ. His revelations through life gave to us the understanding of the heavens and the virtues we all take to God upon our demise. From this, Earth teaches all about darkness and light and the *balancing act* we all undertake with each other.

Our lives are truly a miracle, weaving and sewing our virtues within the *cloth of gold* upon the shoulders of humanity. So in metaphor to truly quench the thirst of knowledge is a cup that is empty and needs to be replenished every day of our existence in life. Thus, each day we awaken from our sleep we SEE our world as an adventure and learning process with life. The rationale of us all should be quietly honourable and discerning about our brethren and sisters of life. Our love is unconditional within heavenly realms and thus our journey in life is once more to seek and find that love which truly exists with virtue.

This new book will bring many bible quotations and the aspects of teaching from ancient to modern times. For we as humanity will learn about our *Universal Fellowship and the SEE of life* with love and compassion with magnitude and God.

Our Earth is the elemental reasoning of spiritual resonance and through life we experience her assets and gifts. These gifts have been born through evolution and spin. The retrograde aspect is that truthfully lessons about greed, desire, hate, anger, tyranny and desolation of hope are still prevalent within our world societies today. We still maintain the have and have not. People preserve their fortunes and luxuries without realising the suffering of global inequality. Despite our intelligences and science predictions about the Cosmos, we have yet to understand the realities of *Divine Science* and the progress we have yet to make as humanity.

Thus, our learning with appreciation and wisdom begins with this book.

Beautiful Bath and Malmesbury
May 2013

Elizabeth Jane Parker

A trip to Bath Spa, a sojourn in May
Inclement weather is on display
The clouds darken with Spartan blue
The snaky wind chills us, biting too
This however does not deter
Enjoying the break we can refer
The sights and sounds of history around
The majestic impression is very profound
Visitors from around the Globe
Fascinated by the beauty exposed
With Yellow Stone of Regency build
Before the Saxons and Romans instilled
Their mark in time for us to know
History, fascination our journeys to go

The Romans Baths discovered beneath
Their mystery hidden is our bequeath
The Waters that bathed centuries ago
Up from the Earth they still bestow
Bubbling deep from the Earth's core
The heat will come evermore
The historic atmosphere is omnipresent
With people, places and The Crescent
Magnificent gardens neatly deferential
A must visit is omnipotent and essential
Birds everywhere and in song,

Singing joyfully, echoes are strong
The perfume of flowers elegantly arrayed
Iridescent splendour artistically displayed
For admiration for all to see
Bath definitely is a place to be

The canal, a hidden gem for us to go
The sign of spring the water does flow
Barge Boats, Cyclists, Swans, and Ducks with young
Add to the canvass our sight has begun
Beautiful gardens come down to the edge
Box topiary formed into a hedge
Allotments growing, produce and food
To look and observe but not to intrude
The backs of houses upon the hill
With elevation, marvel and articulate skill

The memories are strong in this city of old
The Museum, a building majestic to behold
With artefacts of beauty, elegance and design
The porcelain and pictures with colours define
That mankind has a marvellous gift
Inventions and creations to simply uplift
How proud we can be with God's loving grace
The wonder of life for us all to embrace

The open top bus, is a must to make
Interestingly panoramic for all to take
A city and countryside all around
The views, the commentary will astound
This place so grand we can recall
The visitor's interest is ne'er so small

Everywhere you can see nature, city and creation
Of man's intelligence and generation
We can all share this, with wonder to decide
England's inheritance, history and pride

The Peregrine Falcon, nesting upon the Church Spire
People sitting on the bench we enquire
The man with binoculars lets us see
Closely at these birds, that is bountifully free
The symbolism of God with hawk and living
A nesting box the church is giving
Two babies survive, she comes each year
To Bath, to breed and to rear
Her young to live and generate a time
For a future with nature and the sublime

Our next visit is to Malmesbury at "The Old Bell"
With ghost stories, ancient history to tell
Wisteria grows upon the walls
The blue flower with perfume gently falls
The historic Abbey sits next door
Waiting patiently for us to explore

The Naked Gardeners of television renown
Built a garden in the Abbey grounds
The countryside and Malmesbury itself
Virtually and island upon a shelf
Of Hills and meadows circulating around
Famous, interesting it will astound
Fields of yellow buttercups cause us to stop
Walking observing their magnanimous crop

*Butterflies with orange tips can be seen
Their presence so pretty and serene
Mallard ducks with young to survive
Nature's predators and man's gun, do they hide
Swans upon nests incubating their young
And despite wind chill there is some Sun
We espy a Yellow Wagtail upon the stream
Reflecting and dainty, so serene
The bridges of Malmesbury take us over water
From Ancient times do not alter
For passage and symbolism to replace
The steps of life we all retrace*

*Dark clouds formulate upon our walk
We meet a man and engage in talk
The beautiful town of Malmesbury to see
Wiltshire in England, a place to be
Absorbing our sights and sounds of time
Memories forever can define
That the Cosmic Entrancement and the big SEE
Captivates our thoughts and time entity*

*The message of life is appreciate this
To Walk the Earth can be bliss
With caring and sharing this planet of ours
To make peace within the consequent hours
Minutes and seconds of our lives
With God in our hearts always strives
To believe and know that he is around
Listen and learn with sight and sound
The metamorphoses within the spectrum
The turning Earth the resurrection*

Belief is powerful with virtue and love
God shows this when we know from above
That all of creation is an adventure with time
The waters of life will define
That the treasures of life bring humanity this
In seeking and learning discoveries of bliss
The Amalgamation of truth
The assimilation of bio chemistry
The objectivity of purpose
The knowledge and the love
That God abounds of us all
For evermore

Amen

Chapter One

The Connection and Vibration of Truth

"Ye have heard that it has been said, An eye for an eye, and a tooth for a tooth; but I say unto you, that ye who resist evil; but whoever shall smite thee on the right cheek, turn to him the other also. And if any man shall sue thee at law, and take away thy coat, let thee have thy cloak also."

St Matthew 5 : 38-40

THE LOVE OF GOD *is about us all* truly understanding and seeking with our journey through life and reasoning. The emphasis for us all is to learn about each generation and transition with Earth and Heavenly vibration. The wonders and attributes of mankind is indeed a miracle with time and life. We as yet as humanity have not learnt about the vibrations of cosmic entrancement with science and biology understanding and coping with darkness. Each day for us should be a learning experience with God and his Holy Angels showing us all about our divine one. The culmination across the globe at present is distorted belief and tyranny in the name of God our creator of virtue and reasoning.

CHAPTER ONE

We live and learn through the transitional metaphysics and realism of our Planet Earth. For she gives to us all unconditionally. But still we take and take without consideration for her generosity. We take for granted the wonder of timescale and challenge. We take for granted the gifts of God to man and his intelligence. We take for granted the beauty and the darkness of our souls. For to learn and process with eternal spin is to grow and prosper with life's journey with God by our side.

Stand still, and consider the wondrous works of God.
Dost thou know when God disposed them?
And caused the light of his cloud to shine?
Dost thou know the balancing of the clouds?
The wondrous works of him which is perfect in knowledge?

Job 37 : 14-16

This part of the Holy Bible could well have been written by William Shakespeare; however, one must assume the connection and beauty of the written word. As with another William, *"to walk lonely as a cloud"* – why then spiritually are we all fascinated with the concept of hydrodynamics? Poetically and scientifically they bring us life and inspiration. This simple analogy brings us again to wonder at the beauty of this phenomenon and the life-giving properties this element contains for us in life.

> *Remember that thou magnify his work,*
> *Which men behold*
> *Every man may see it;*
> *Man may behold it afar off.*
> *Behold, God is great, and we know him not,*
> *Neither can the number of his years be searched out.*
> *For he maketh small drops of water:*
> *They pour down rain according to the vapour thereof:*
> *Which clouds do drop*
> *And distil upon man abundantly.*

Job 36 : 24-28

From this passage the beauty of the words were written many centuries past before the understanding of modern science, but it was understood by education of those times that clouds were indeed vaporous. Inspiration from clouds is an essential part of our lives but through the writings of bygone people we find beauty and enlightenment for both our spirit and our soul.

To see and feel GOD is a message of life and meaning through all of the wonders of Earth, and the universal energies which give to us a life with intelligence and biology. This miracle is to be believed every day of our life and to know that through the reality of living we can know our Earth and our God in Heaven. For Earth is part of the heavenly process and through her eternal spin and evo-devo functioning we walk with God and life.

Appreciation is a word humanity needs to simplify with everyday comforts and needs. For through this elemental extraneous focus point we can find humility as humanity for our bearing and status in life and reasoning.

> *I will praise thee, O Lord, with my whole heart:*
> *I will shew forth all thy marvellous works,*
> *I will be glad and rejoice in thee:*
> *I will sing praise to thy name, O thou most High.*

Psalm 9 : 1-2

And God so loved the Earth he gave his only Son and from these words from the Holy Bible we have to appreciate the wondrous teachings of *Jesus Christ our Lord*. Thus, to follow his footsteps was to lead humanity into the arms of God and his wondrous beauty. Also, to appreciate that our lives will form many contradictions with the societies of the world is to understand that the deep meaning of our soul is to seek the *Glory of God and his love of our Earth*. Through Jesus Christ we came to know about eternal love and destination and through our spiritual journey we came to know his love for us all. Blessings are eternal knowledge with the lessons of humanity and the Way of the Lord.

Back to basics again, is to understand the miracle and the symbolic cup of life. Yes, water. The beginning of life began with water, and did Jesus himself not only walk upon it but taught us all to appreciate the properties of hydrodynamics and God our Father? So the *Holy Water* again, a symbol through the *Established Church* which sanctifies, heals and inspires us all through reality and reasoning with our Earth. We as endocrines with life are about the holy association with Jesus through the cup of life and the blood of Christ shed for us all to find salvation both in life and death. Through the eternal *Holy Spirit* we understand our faith is the reasoning of life through the maze of misconception and downfall. For the LORD speaks to us all when we hear as with Galatians 5 : 1 –

Stand fast therefore in the liberty wherewith Christ hath made us free, and be not entangled again with the yoke of bondage.

Every day we understand our connections with light and traverse the mountain of truth with believing in the righteous messages of GOD. Through the evil prevalent within our world we truly overcome the bonds of hatred with love. For is love not the purification and virtue of energies curtailing our path with influence? Through *Holy Scripture* we can all find some answers for our doubts and the influence of dark clusters circumnavigating our globe to this very day.

The Divine Reality is about virtue and love overcoming all ill intent from our brethren and sisters of life who have not found GOD and his messages of hope, love and valour. In a modern world of dispute and dilemma those seeking God should feel welcome and without the confinement of monetary gain within *Established Places of Worship*. Throughout the concept of modern monism, for those people who seek knowledge and inspiration will gladly give and share with all the wondrous works of life and fellowship as was intended as a holy message from all divine prophets and messengers of light. The free will of GOD is about the freedom and elevation of the Holy Spirit for all who truly follow the way.

For this cause I bow my knees unto the Father of our LORD Jesus Christ,
Of whom the whole family in heaven and earth is named,
That he will grant you, according to the riches of glory,
To be strengthened with might by his Spirit in the inner man:
That Christ may dwell in your hearts by faith, being rooted and grounded
In love

Ephesians 3 : 14-17

Lesson

Wherefore laying aside all malice, and all guile and hypocrisies, and envies and all evil speakings, as newborn babes, desire the sincere milk of the word, that ye may grow thereby: if so be ye have tasted that the Lord is gracious.

I Peter 2 : 1-3

*   *   *

WE AS HUMANITY live upon the Earth with *the foundation stone* of senses and coercion with all living things. We breathe, we learn and we grow from our senses and GOD-given intelligence. This is another simplification of life and gift from Heaven with Earth. Our confessional relationship with dark energies is to know that true love is the greatest enemy of evil. So from this analogy we as fellowship need to learn and understand our choices in life are based upon virtue and love showing us the way forward with GOD our Father and his love for us all to cherish our lives no matter what.

Impermanence is a truth and from yesterday we leave behind the memories of good and bad circulating with our spirit and soul. But we learn from our LORD Jesus Christ that our lives are eternal with the understanding of virtue and love as a guide.

* * *

> *Beloved, think it not strange concerning the fiery trial which is to try you, as though some strange thing happened unto you: but rejoice inasmuch as ye are partakers of Christ's sufferings; that when his glory shall be revealed, ye may be glad also with exceeding joy. If you are reproached for the name of Christ, happy are ye; for the spirit of glory and of God resteth upon you.*
>
> *I Peter 4 : 12-14*

* * *

CHAPTER ONE

The beauty of this from the *Holy Bible* indicates that through Jesus Christ and his suffering he demonstrated to us through understanding that life can be cruel but from our learning we can truly believe and learn from our existence that, no matter what, GOD brings us eternal life and that he does not forsake us through eternal spirit and life as one. For to know our LORD is to know that he brought us teachings and love from the Heavens. And through him and his disciples the beauty of life and reasoning will exonerate all other downfalls with our belief and trust with GOD.

From our journey through life we must always know that choices are about our individualism. To understand our individualism is to know that we are never alone with the Holy Spirit by our side. Belief is powerful when we understand that virtue and love appertain to GOD only and through our pathway we can find him always with our virtue.

* * *

> *Be patient therefore, brethren, unto the coming of the LORD. Behold, the husbandman waiteth for the precious fruit of the earth, and hath long patience for it, until he receive the early and latter rain. Be ye also patient; stablish your hearts: for the coming of the LORD draweth nigh.*
>
> *James 5 : 7-8*

* * *

We as fellowship must learn compassion; wisdom and love are the assets GOD gives to us all without judgement. Choices are heaven-sent when we follow our individualism and our singular virtuous choices without influence. The Holy Spirit is about guidance with virtuous intent only and is available to us all when in need. For our choices belong to ownership and through ownership we learn about the realities of life and the wonder of the Holy Spirit.

Thus, the cup of life needs to be replenished each day of our lives with humility, honour and respect of all living things. Through this we can be inspired about ownership, nirvana and earth as one element of intelligence and knowledge. The humanitarian cup of knowledge is never full and each day we learn to replenish our belief, our love and truth through this cup. Our thirst in metaphor will be quenched each evening we retire and our knowledge will be our achievement with understanding the precious jewel of life. For life is a reason for giving, receiving and loving.

* * *

Let no man say when he is tempted, I am tempted of God:
for God cannot be tempted with evil.

James 1 : 13

Chapter Two

Hark! The Herald Angels Sing

O give thanks to the Lord; call upon his name:
Make known his deeds among people.
Sing unto him, sing psalms unto him:
Talk ye of all his wondrous works.
Glory ye in his holy name:
Let the heart of them rejoice that seek the LORD

Psalm 105 : 1-3

WE AS HUMANITY have grown from time immortal through elements of wind, rain, fire, molten rock and geographical disturbances of great capacity. We as humanity have deliberated and wondered at our Universal Scriptures with God at the helm. We as humanity have learnt and re-learnt about life, biology and Earth.

How do we truly understand LORD Jesus Christ as a man of learning, teaching and living as a divine spirit among the peoples of the world?

> *Seek the Lord, and his strength:*
> *Seek his face evermore.*
> *Remember his marvellous works that he hath done:*
> *His wonders and the judgements of his mouth*

Psalm 105 : 4-5

The propulsion of virtuous energies with life and biology is the miracle of vehicle and decision within a body of light. This body of light is about appreciation and understanding the messages of Angels and God through universal structure and igniting the *fire of knowledge* precipitated by virtuous energies maintaining philosophy and psychic union with Heaven.

> *And Jesus went about all Galilee, teaching in their synagogues, preaching the gospel of the Kingdom, and healing all manner of sickness and all manner of disease among people.*

Matthew 4 : 23

So from our lives how do we understand the values of virtue and love? For Jesus Christ, our LORD gave unconditional love and countenance to those in need. All men and women who heard his teachings began to understand the value of life, reasoning, love, fellowship and GOD. They began to listen and procreate the lessons he gave about respect, love and honour to all those who truly seek the light and love of the Universe – *our Heaven and Earth connection.*

Mankind is yet to see his connection with God and truth being divine love and honour with the path of reality and life itself. From our evangelical beginnings unto the journey of enlightenment our spiritual unification is always following resonance with God and the truth of life and immortality with light. In this Jesus Christ taught the reality of darkness into light and the immersion of our soul into the path of knowledge, honour, righteousness and love.

> *Ask, and it shall be given to you: seek, and ye shall find; knock and it will be opened unto you: for everyone that asketh receiveth; and he that seeketh findeth; and him that knocketh it shall be opened.*
>
> ### *Matthew 7 : 7-8*

Our soul as humanity is eternally seeking the challenges of life but to find our virtue and honour is the *Universal Strategy* finding and maintaining our status quo with God and his Angels. Despite the evil doers of our world great changes can occur for our individualism and soul uniting with Heaven and the messages of virtue and intent when we truly believe and absorb the teachings of the Way. We only truly understand when we believe in honour and love. Thus, the immortality and spiritual migration through biological transition and journey is to understand our connection with great Masters and union with God through their teachings and wisdom with light.

The Inspiration of Cambridgeshire
Elizabeth Jane Parker

The beauty of eternal light

Living the dream with reality in flight
A pretty village of ancient stone
Through history 1649, would have known
Remove the cars and tarmac too
Back in time you can imbue
The imagination of a time gone by
Historian records you can rely
A coaching inn for travellers to the North
Relying on hostelry for their course

Today a walk along the River Nene
So much nature to be seen
A beautiful bridge takes us across
Bath Stone and splendour with time to emboss
Horses grazing in the field
Swishing flies and wearing a shield
Along the muddy path we go
The River Nene with heavy flow
Following a path indicated by signs
We appreciate the beauty of countryside finds

CHAPTER TWO

Dragonflies searching to procreate
Their species forever symbolises fate
Damsel flies of bright beautiful blue
Skimming the water and reeds; of colourful hue
The path of conservation is clearly signed
Searching to see the beauty refined
The recent rains have caused some floods
The river banks swollen emitting their muds
A heron flies along the bank so low
His velocity with nature is to know
The balance of life refreshes evolution
Giving us hope for tomorrow's resolution

A Kestrel flutters for its prey
And high in the sky a Red Kite on display
Skimming the thermals with elegant ease
Searching for carrion so he can feed
Rare butterflies are seen upon the wing
A multitude of grasshoppers gratefully sing
A Robin flies into the trees
Upon a warm day of glorious breeze
Everywhere we look we see the beauty of creation
Everywhere we walk, we absorb Earth's vibration
For the richness of life upon the crown of gold
Truly is free for us to behold
The jewels of life is the treasure to us all
From GOD'S creation from large unto small

Wild geese sit upon the grass so proud
Haughty in stature, their honking so loud!
The weir makes musicality and water to fall
Into the river the sea will call
For rainclouds always calling it home

HARK! THE HERALD ANGELS SING

Down to the shores gravity has shown
The way of hydrosphere brings us all life
To enjoy
To embrace
To know
To appreciate
Always GOD'S Grace

We all awaken to this every day
With knowledge, adventure and something to say
The virtues of yesterday impinge on our minds
To seek with renewal our fundamental finds
The LOVE OF GOD is to be known
Through angels of light this will be shown
The grey sky of early morn has gone
The birds are happily in their song
Of melodies of change and vibration
Knowing these times will become celebration

The beauty of knowledge showing the way
That despite the evil our World can display
The wonders of life and being with GOD
Into our hearts the soil of Earth and the sod
For today we can all begin again and
The journey continues where love will remain
The cup of knowledge to satisfy our souls
Borne with humility,
Borne with honour
Borne with truth
Borne with love
Forever

Chapter Three

The Fruits of Wisdom

If any of you lack wisdom, let him ask of GOD that giveth to all men liberally, and upbraideth not: and it shall be given to him. But let him ask in faith, nothing wavering.

James 1 : 5-6

HOW DO WE actually understand and appreciate wisdom, likened to the fruit of the Earth? Wisdom has been the very foundation of many beliefs but as yet mankind needs to learn and proactivate this. Wisdom is indeed a science of compassion, honour and truth. The inspiration of this is a blessing and instrumentation of passage with virtue. Virtue is the flower in bloom. Geometrically and realistically, our individual aura will carry light into the pathway of knowledge and love. Humanitarian intelligence is about the simplicity of wisdom but the complication of challenge — challenge to our virtues through life and reasoning.

Let brotherly love continue

Hebrews 13 : 1

Did our Lord Jesus Christ not suffer and perish as a man through the bonds of tyranny? And through the cruelty and the ultimate price of humanity he showed us his virtues and dedication to GOD.

*   *   *

Whosoever believeth that Jesus is the Christ is born of GOD, and every one that loveth him that begat loveth him also that is begotten of him. By this we know that we love the children of GOD, when we love GOD, and keep his commandments.

The Holy Bible
(1 John 5 : 1-2)

*   *   *

Today in our modern world there are many misunderstandings about religion the beauty and knowledge this brings to us all. Our LORD Jesus Christ gave to us his learning and knowledge with wisdom, love and honour. And despite his virtue he was persecuted by those who were HOLY. Why?

*   *   *

CHAPTER THREE

Beloved, if GOD so loved us, we ought also to love one another. No man has seen GOD at any time. If we love one another, GOD dwelleth in us, and his love is perfected in us. Hereby know we that we dwell in him, and he in us, because he hath given us his Spirit. And we have seen and do testify that the Father sent the SON to be the Saviour of the World.

I John 4 : 11-14

* * *

The love of God is about true love of the Holy Spirit and involves us all should we so wish to learn and understand the virtuous wisdom of the ALMIGHTY GOD our father. And through Jesus Christ his virtuous way was to bring peace, love and honour to all.

* * *

And this is his commandment that we should believe on the name of his SON Jesus Christ, and love one another, as he gave us commandment, and he that keepeth his commandments dwelleth in him, and he in him. And hereby we know that he abideth in us, by the Spirit which he has given us.

I John 3 : 23-24

* * *

Again, we ask the question about world peace and the belief in GOD that many religions and creeds believe in. We do not have any records available today of Jesus and his thoughts about this but the words from the Bible are thus:

> *For whatsoever is born of GOD overcometh the world: and this is the victory that overcometh the world, even our faith. Who is he that overcometh the world, but he that believeth that Jesus is the Son of God? This is he that came by water and blood, even Jesus Christ; not by water only, but by water and blood. And it is the Spirit that beareth witness, because the spirit is truth.*
>
> **I John 5 : 4-6**

*   *   *

Our modern brotherhood and sisterhood with life is now one of worldwide knowledge about creed and belief. How do we believe Jesus would have spoken of GOD and the wonder of his wisdom today?

> *If we receive the witness of men, the witness of GOD is greater: for this is the witness of GOD which he has testified of his SON.*
>
> **1 John 5 : 9**

CHAPTER THREE

* * *

The messages to our LORD were indeed about honour, but the recognition of his begotten SON was to teach us all about the values and love of humanity. For the LORD of Heavens brought his love and teachings to us all to follow by choice.

* * *

We know that whosoever is born of GOD sinneth not; but he that is begotten of GOD keepeth himself, and that wicked one touches him not.

1 John 5 : 18

* * *

God sent his son to us, as men and women to seek and find the glory of our father and creator with heavens. However, today science would teach us otherwise and so in this modern world for people to actually SEE the reality of our LORD and his messages to us as humanity is a minefield of media, interpretation and materialism. How do we today portray his love and virtue from 2000 years ago? We once again come to prayer, and request the true meaning of virtue and love. We seek to know more about a man who gave his life for us. We seek his knowledge, aspirations and love of life. We seek his foundation with Earth and his whole life from man and boy. We seek his eternal love.

Wisdom Personified

THE OVERRIDING FACTOR with GOD is the virtuous aspect of learning and intent. Many people fail to actually see themselves and the responsibility of ownership and the living miracle both within the realms of spirituality and biology. Intelligence is the aspect of wisdom with science and from this understanding and perspective we begin to SEE the reality of life and know that we exist within a vast UNIVERSE. Our individual UNIVERSE is but a small speck of dust within the reformation of multifarious beliefs and transitions of a Universe within a Universe and the smallest light shining within magnitude brings a diorama of beauty and colour when we as humanity understand virtue and all aspects of faith.

Our Earth is the shining example of evolution and change through eons of imperceptive transition. Her diametric proportions are but a minute astrological zodiac within a vast expanse of time and space. To know this is to know that learning is eternal and no matter how Science perceives factual elements and theory, the relativity of our lives relies upon the simple effects of hydrosphere and water. Our spiritual aspect is the purification of human weakness through understanding our soul's journey through biology. No matter what we are we can all find our reality and reason with love showing us the way from dishonour and anger. For anger is indeed a poison which even when diluted can bring mayhem to ownership. The true beauty of love is the ultimate forgiveness through time and space.

> *But the wisdom that is from above is first pure, then peaceable, gentle, and easy to be intreated, full of mercy and good fruits without partiality, and without hypocrisy. And the fruit of righteousness is sown in peace of them that make peace.*
>
> **James 3 : 17-18**

Our LORD Jesus Christ was a preacher and teacher of wisdom

*   *   *

> *Glory to God in the highest, and on Earth peace, good will toward all men.*
> **Luke 2 : 14**

* * *

From this we as humanity work with all positive elements of the Holy Bible to entrust the blessings and love from the Heavens. The truth of our LORD was with purity and light with all of the Holy Covenants expressing the virtues of life and reason with realistic components from the Word. The true wisdom of the Heavens is to know in metaphor that we can for ever eat the fruit and plant the seed of Divine Love. For love and honour to ourselves and that of our Earth we for ever learn to appreciate the fruits and the bread of life.

* * *

And as they did eat, Jesus took bread, and blessed, and brake it, and gave to them and said, "Take, eat: this is my body." And he took the cup, and when he had given thanks, he gave it to them: and they drank it.

Mark 14 : 22

* * *

The beauty of this token is to demonstrate appreciation of food and drink for us as humanity and the LORD proclaimed his humanity to humanity. His flesh and blood was a gift to us all through the beauty of his eternal soul and the fruits of Earth as he is our soul's sustenance with The Christ and with GOD our father. His symbolism was about the virtue of gift and life through our Earth and her gifts to us in life, and in death do we find our truth once more within the realms of Divinity and Heaven.

From all things in life our choices with both modern and ancient lineage is to understand our mortality within the realms of co-existence with Earth and her gifts. Jesus understood this and through his reverence to *Mother Earth* he gave the gift of life to all people who believe in him. And from him he gave his life blood and sacrificed his beauty and reverence with life itself. He understood the miracle of all things from the Universe and his Jewish belief encompassed the true love of GOD our father over all mercies and faith.

*   *   *

> *The light of the body is the eye: therefore when thine eye is single, thy whole body also is full of light: but when thine eye is evil, thy body also is full of darkness... If thy whole body therefore be full of light, having no part dark, the whole body shall be full of light, as when the bright shining of a candle doth give thee light.*
>
> **Luke 11 : 34-36**

* * *

We know as humanity that the Earth revolves upon her axis around the Cosmos. From this perception with our imagination and scientific revelation we as mankind are not as understanding of Universal brotherhood and theism as an element of teaching our spiritual light upon Earth. The light of us all is currently not conducive to a coaxial of knowledge and light understanding respect, honour and truth as yet. So, to know that the past has been both a celestial sphere and living containment within biology we have as societies not understood the beauty and love of our GOD and his prophets whatever creed or faith upon Earth. We need to know that our intelligence is powerful and creative but through this, our modern society is fragmenting the wonder of life and the connections of our Universe as one. This may seem unbelievable but we are all souls of light. Our light is to learn about the adventure and spiritual journey with life.

Beyond an insular world is a parallel Universe which as yet we as mankind have not found but believed through our religions and faith. The true meaning of GOD has been used as ammunition for greed, hate, dishonour, murder and tyranny. This is a sad truth of human history.

We all seem to accept the world we live in but complain about our brethren. All lives are gifts from Heaven and even evil can be dissimulated when we believe in the beauty of our Earth and her gifts to us in life. This is where we learn again from the ashes of hope. The electromotive forces of the Universe is to be explained again for us all on

Earth so we may pick up the threads of *celestial gold* and sew our future path with GOD and grace for betterment.

So we begin.

*   *   *

> *The judgements of the LORD are true and righteous altogether.*
> *More to be desired are they than gold, yes much more than fine gold:*
> *Sweeter than honey and the honeycomb*
> *Moreover by them is the servant warned:*
> *And keeping of them is great reward*

Psalm 19 : 9-11

The Winding Steps

Elizabeth Jane Parker

Upon the winding steps of life
We negotiate the upturns and the strife
The impending steps of those before
We gradually step on to each floor
To rest upon the turrets of time
The meeting of Angels into sublime
Looking through glass; a window to see
A landscape so large… eternal to be

We as humanity walk with the Earth
From ending to beginnings we have rebirth
Always available from lessons of hope
Despite the challenges set to cope
We are reaching for the stars
God to see our light
God to know our One
God to know us all
We live, we teach, we love and chance
From God's creation we have perchance;
To obtain
The knowledge bestowed no matter who we are
That elusive light within our star
Earth and beauty is so strange
Reaching our destination; is always arranged
Through learning,
Understanding
And being our light...
The wonder of the Eagle in Flight
To know that we are blessed indeed
Following his virtue, love and creed

The message of Angels comes to us all
The light of learning is never so small
The mountain of truth is there to be seen
For the SEE of life; his knowledge has been
The eternal message of faith and journey
To maintain our path with God's will and proof
To give us all a journey with truth
That he loves unconditionally for us to feel
The sight and light will always reveal
The words of wisdom giving us strength
That we will walk at any length

CHAPTER THREE

The Earth with her mysterious past
Into a future, magnitude and vast
Of humanity and intelligence being us all
A story of the Christlight to recall

The History of devotion to God
That Jesus Christ his feet have trod
Through a maze of life and age of reason
Against his being there was treason
But again we come to light the way
And now our God will have his say
About philanthropy being at one
The feet of all humanity now begun
With
Acknowledgement
Acceptance
Forbearance
Determination
Love
Honour
Truth
With GOD by our side
Forever

Chapter Four

The Lord of Truth

The meek shall eat and be satisfied:
They shall praise the LORD that seek him:
Your heart shall live forever.
All the ends of the World shall remember and turn to the
LORD:
And all the kindreds of the Nations shall worship before thee.

Psalm 22 : 26-27

TO REASON THE FUTURE is about mankind overcoming the desires of materialism, greed, debt, gluttony, delusion and destruction. For the LORD teaches us all about contentment, honour, love and conveniences of sharing the World and her gifts to us all in life.

The wicked borroweth, and payeth not again:
But the righteous sheweth mercy, and giveth.
For such as be blessed of him shall inherit the Earth.

Psalm 37 : 21-22

CHAPTER FOUR

From this speculation and analogy we as modern humanity must understand the realities of sustenance and the geographical limitation for resources. At present our *Leaders* concentrate on the economy. However; *economical* is a non-descriptive accuracy when we understand that our world is rich and diverse with natural life and is irretrievably beautiful when we learn to SEE and know our spiritual connection with life does not involve money. So to understand our faith and belief in hope is the necessary attribute of today. For our hope and valour with the *Cosmological Vibration with Earth* is to know that we will overcome the blindness of tantalising materialism and wealth. GOD and the vibration of virtue are the most powerful reasoning and love of all.

The blind alleys to which our societies are being led bring no satisfaction from desire and materialism. The onward march for mankind is spiralling with impatient vertigo with assets accumulating material wealth and non-distribution of love, compassion and generosity towards our Earth, ourselves and life for the future. Is this currently a truth or fact about our modern world?

I waited patiently for the LORD
And he inclined unto me, and heard my cry
He brought me up also out of a horrible pit,
Out of miry clay,
And set my feet upon a rock and established my goings.
He hath put a new song in my mouth,
Even praise unto our GOD.

Psalm 40 : 1-3

The wonder of life and meaning is about our responsibility as humanity and our worship of GOD our father in Heaven. To believe and realise that we are not alone through life when we believe and understand the wonder of all things made from GOD our Father and creator.

Blessed is the man that maketh the LORD
his trust
Psalm 40 : 4

The absolutisms of life ever increase with virtuous intentions following the way of the blessed. All avenues through life can lead to GOD when we simply follow the signs of forgiveness and love. However, our modern world currently seeks to find the creation of wealth against the validation of contentment. So to know GOD becomes one of blinding misconceptions. The simplicity of life becomes a complication for many to SEE and the relief aspect of love and forgiveness are often overridden with darkness and anger. So we learn from the Bible as thus:

Praise waiteth for thee, O God, in Sion:
Unto thee shall the vow be performed.
O thou hearest my prayer,
Unto thee shall all flesh come.
Iniquities prevail against me:
As for our transgressions, thou shalt purge them away.

CHAPTER FOUR

Blessed is the man or woman thou choosest,
And causest to approach unto thee,
That he may dwell in thy courts;
We shall be satisfied with the goodness of thy house
Even in thy Holy Temple.

Psalm 65 : 1-4

Chapter Five

The sanctification of virtue

Blessed be the GOD and Father of our Lord Jesus Christ, who has blessed us with all Spiritual Blessings in heavenly places in Christ: according as he hath chosen us in him before the foundation of the World, that we should be holy and without blame before him in love.

Ephesians 1 : 3-4

THE LOVE AND FOUNDATION *of our LORD* was spoken many centuries ago through the divine channel. How have we understood this during the *twenty-first century?* For every person alive today, 29th September 2012, we are all upon a primeval agenda through life and reasoning. As has been said before, we all walk upon the Earth with this knowledge and the simplicity of our journey both with spirit and with biology is to know that we are this. Our modern age has become a dilemma of purpose with life and GOD our Father; for his reasoning is the eternal knowledge we all seek to know in mortality but to carry our virtuous understanding with love.

And that, knowing the time, that now it is high time to awake out of sleep; for now is our salvation nearer than we believed. The night is far spent, the day is

CHAPTER FIVE

at hand: let us cast off the works of darkness, and let us put on the amour of light. Let us walk honestly, as in the day: not in rioting or drunkenness, not in chambering and wantonness, not in strife or envying.

Romans 13 : 11-13

Our World today is still without truth, love and honour among all the followers of GOD and his love for humanity. Mankind has yet to bring his understanding unto Earth with humility, honour and belief. Our Lord of the Heavens does not deprive us of joy and laughter. For this is indeed a message we all have with GOD, but from our modern age we have developed once more into the diachronic aspects *of somnambulism* with our Earth and her beauty with truth.

In order for us all to understand the perspective and prospectus of *Divine Love* is to know the darkness that follows our soul, but to know that we can all disperse the phrenology of hatred, greed, malicious intent, anger, travesty and desire with love, honour and truth lighting our passage with divine discernment with determination and free will with God by our side. We can all find our salvation and contentment within life and limitations of biological containment upon our path of individual learning. Love is the most powerful and beautiful aspect of our learning through life and journey and thus we all find our strength with the hidden assets of devotion through God and his followers with truth. We as humanity have indeed forgotten our purpose within a world of sharing and caring for each other. Our brother and sisters of *Billions* no longer aspire to a World that is wonder and quintessentially devoted to Earth and each other.

> *Wherefore receive ye one another, as Christ also received us to the Glory of God.*
>
> ***Romans 15 : 7***

> *Now the GOD of hope fill you with all joy and peace in believing, that ye may abound in hope, through the power of the HOLY GHOST. And I am persuaded of you, my brethren, that ye also are full of goodness, filled with all knowledge, able also to admonish one another.*
> ***Romans 15 : 13-14***

The wisdom of GOD is the eternal message to us all in life to pursue our lives with love and virtuous intent. Laughter and joy are included to us all when we understand life and journey with virtue. Our *GOLD OF UNDERSTANDING* is the divine message of love with the challenges that beset us all with the downfalls and the upturns of our life. To practice what we preach, life is to know that to err is human but to find our path with salvation is the key with forgiveness, truth and motivation to move forward with our light and not the darkness of anger.

> *Who is a wise man and endued with knowledge*

> *among you? Let him shew out of a good
> conversation his works with meekness of wisdom.*
>
> ***James 3 : 13***

Whatever contradictions we may face can indeed be to know that the love of GOD is real and does not judge with contempt. His love for our Earth and humanity are best spoken as thus:

> *He that will love life,*
> *And see good days.*
> *Let him refrain his tongue from evil,*
> *And his lips that they speak no guile:*
> *Let him eschew evil, and do good:*
> *Let him seek peace and ensue it.*
> *For the eyes of the LORD are over the righteous*
> *And his ears are open unto their prayers.*
>
> ***I Peter 3 : 10-12***

Aspirations
Elizabeth Jane Parker

> **Autumn's gold** *is upon us once more*
> *A visit to Stratford is a journey before*
> *William Shakespeare playwright, Poet*
> *And a lay preacher for God*

THE SANCTIFICATION OF VIRTUE

A wander through Stratford he would have trod
His personality shines within his word
Inspirationally a genius, today he is heard
Globally famous with worship to date
His presence as a writer does also relate
In the absence of words he invented some more
Now the Oxford Dictionary we can explore
His marvellous mind and words he contained
1700 we use today, eloquently maintained

William Shakespeare *gave us his gift*
Speeches and words for us to uplift
A theatre of actors upon the stage
Throwing their voices upon a charade
Devotion to words and projective description
Playing the part, a masquerade of inscription
Of words written simply designed to entertain
With heart-to-heart; ne-r does refrain
From a performance entertaining and passionately grand
We sit with wonder in the stand
To inspire the mind with significance and fun
A tale of mystery has begun
Laughter, poignancy and sadly tragic
His words giving deliverance and magic

*"***Alas, poor Yorick***" the Actor does say*
From a character he will emphatically display
The invented story of tragedy and drama
Giving us fascination, description and panorama

As with Stratford *a town of history*
Visitors will come for a remarkable mystery

CHAPTER FIVE

Of stories told about his life and story
His ongoing name with plays of glory
We can all enjoy his eternal fame
In England his birthplace and famous name
His continuity of placement will always live on
Through education, interest and where he belonged

From shores afar *and near, people come*
To visit his birthplace of brilliance undone
Photos taken, questions asked
About this man and his past
Gift shops, Shakespeare's house and surrounding town
People surge from all around
To know a man of infinite popularity
Upon the stage and familiarity
The wonder of word and speech to recite
The wonder of William Shakespeare
The wonder of Stratford-upon-Avon
The wonder of humanity
The wonder of seeing and believing
Just simply the wonder...

Fascination is a word *or us all*
History, philosophy we can recall
The magic of word and descriptive production
We today enjoy the reproduction
Of the mind of people who have been and passed
Into the light of redemption surpassed
William Shakespeare a man of God and thought
His gift in life was a story he sought
To entertain and his mind of genius dexterity
Giving his actors to tell of perplexity

Thus we are entertained and told
The aspirations from his pen unfold
Aspirations of God
Aspirations of all
Aspirations of eternal love and friendship
Aspirations of humour
Aspirations of mystery
Aspirations of faith
Aspirations of our past
Aspirations of life and love

Sanctification & Virtue

Elizabeth Jane Parker

THE SANCTIFICATION OF VIRTUE *during our modern age* is to understand our soul incarnate and our life with Earth and her compounds of scientific reasoning with resonance. Our world as humanity has not been systematically dialectic with philanthropic respect. We have all attempted to *overshadow each other* and often fail to SEE the beauty of mankind and his wondrous gifts with intelligence. Understanding is the greatest asset with knowledge and progression along spiritual paths. The complication for us all is through dialect, disrespect and materialism servicing our modern desires to one-upmanship with modern-day reasoning. Our world is a wonder for us all to SEE but through the blindness of misconception and misunderstanding our soul's purpose we all often misdirect our *Way and knowledge with God our Father and Earth Mother*. The purpose of us all in life is to wander along our path of learning and through misdirection find our footing once more with the virtues and teachings of love and justice with angels of all and God of light.

The fantasy aspect of our journey and imagination often imbues us as humanity to wish and desire materialism and money. However, the needs and desires of ownership during our *21st Century* is decreasing our space upon Earth and the marvels of natures and balance for our quadrilateral strength, courage, wisdom and compassion. The smallest part of our creation is to understand the molecules of life and growth. The transition of youth, middle and older is to know that our journey can always be a fascination with life when we choose to SEE the Earth and Heavens as one collaborative with eternity, ecology and evolution. The three "E" element of existence with pantheism, philanthropy and celestial voltage can be understood with humility, honour and heaven and the magnetic storm of light and Earth combining a journey of mysticism, imagination and metaphysics combining as intelligence with GOD and his journey with humanity at the helm is becoming a complication for philanthropic knowledge and truth.

The simplification of intelligence brings us back to the aspects of *Holy Angels* and their kinetic energies through time and space. The believability for us all is about understanding the existence of virtue within celestial spheres and the reality of modern mindset embracing the realities of our eternal father and mother of life itself. Our journey as humanity is a small speck of dust within the oceanic waves of time and from this perspective our impact upon this wonder planet of life has become disorientated with negative elements of monochromatic transition and virtue. *Jesus Christ of the Jewish Nation* gave us his knowledge and love for us all to understand our journey through time upon Earth. His love was philanthropic virtue of the purest vibration.

And the Lord shall be King over all the Earth: and in that day there shall be one LORD and his name as ONE.

Zechariah 14 : 9
Ownership Nirvana Earth

However, belief and love is the power of all things eternal and heavenly domains for us is to know and grow with the *light of Christ himself.* This does not encompass ego, self-interest and destruction; this is about virtue and deliberations with positive impartiality with aspects of progression and balance. Our Lord *Jesus Yashua of the Jewish Nation* brought to us all the truth and messages of GOD. We today must understand his virtues with that of our own and his blood shed for us as humanity. Christianity is borne from all avenues of the Jewish faith and thus the Holy Bible translates as thus. From this aspect we all as mankind need to believe in all things good and understand that life will indeed give us challenges both to our virtue and creditability. However misplaced we become within the Universe we can all call upon Jesus and forsake the messages of ill and shadow projection of our brethren and sisters of life. We can all call upon *Jesus Yashua of the Jewish Nation* and understand that the door is always open should we choose to knock. His availability to us all is about the love of GOD, truth, honour and the love which abounds with virtuous passage and light.

> *Behold, the LORD'S hand is not shortened, that it cannot save; neither is his ear heavy, that it cannot hear.*
>
> ### *Isaiah 59 : 1*

Understanding GOD is about life's ups and downs but finding our path again with faith and love. *Jesus Yashua Christ* was our redeemer through his understanding and knowledge with life and creed. His belief was to love humanity *despite the warts of delusion and evil* growing through the time and space of man's intelligence. He gave to us his *Holy Spirit* and virtue with life and reasoning. So from his strength and courage we can all find him with our ownership upon the *stormy seas of life*. God walks among us every day with the Holy Spirit as our guide. Once we as humanity find our light we can understand all pitfalls of vengeance through dishonour of our sisters and brethren with life.

The true love of our knowledge and light is to move ever forward with God teaching us all. The spiritual element of this becomes a foundation of supreme vibration when our metaphysics transforms the emotional tides of fate into one of courage and virtue. The downside of life is not forever and we must all find our strength with hope, valour and truth. The message of mankind was to be a journey with existence and time teaching us all about our spiritual containment and the practicality of biological adventure.

> *"He that doeth truth cometh to the light, that his deeds may become manifest, that they are wrought in God."*
>
> ***John 3 : 21***

Chapter Six

Divine Divinity

HOW DO WE *in a modern age explain Divine Intervention?* The modern theme for us has become a fragmentation of message, illumination and disbelief. There are many people who embrace the *light of knowledge*. From this we move to interpretation and the aspects of modern mindset. To explain intervention is not easily understood, especially the weaknesses of mankind himself/herself. The doors are often closed to ordinary people who embrace the teachings of so long ago. And from the *Established Church* today we find many empty seats upon the learning of *Christ* and his messages to us all. Many people bring messages and writings from the *Holy Bible* and each one is based on individualisms. To verify the foundation of virtue we all seek with our soul the celestial believability of spiritual ONENESS and containment with GOD our father and creator.

There is so much suffering within our world today. And from this the Holy Spirit is not SEEN or as yet known by modernism. The unity and love of GOD is not apparent within our societies as a whole within the Earth and her spherical journey around the Sun. We as humanity are as brothers and sisters of light within darkness. And the story this day is one of dilemma.

> *I beheld the Earth, and lo it was without form, and void; and the heavens, and they had no light. I beheld the mountains and, lo, they trembled and all the hills moved lightly. I beheld, and lo, there was no man, and all the birds of the heavens had fled.*
>
> ***Jeremiah 4 : 23-25***

This extract from The Holy Bible expresses the *prophet's grief* and his belief that our LORD experienced fierce anger. However, for whatever interpretation we may assume this was indeed a personal feeling he experienced with darkness and desolation. However, take note of Galatians 6 : 1-5 —

> *Brethren, if a man be overtaken in a fault, ye which are spiritual, restore such an one in spirit in the meekness; considering thyself, lest thou also be tempted. Bear ye one another's burdens, and so fulfil the law of Christ. For if a man thinks himself to be something, when he is nothing he deceiveth himself. But let everyone prove his own work, and then shall be rejoicing in him alone and not in another. For every man shall bear his own burden.*

This interpretation would simply infer that GOD is indeed personal and from this we all must abide and placate our bearing within a world of dilemma. However, through *Jesus Yashua Christ* we can find salvation and honour among all peoples of the world and the blessings of Heaven upon Earth.

CHAPTER SIX

From henceforth let no man trouble me, for I bear in my body the marks of Lord Jesus. Brethren, the grace of our LORD Jesus Christ be with your spirit. Amen.

Galatians 6 : 17-18

However, the church has a responsibility to give a powerful message to ordinary people and this does imply that *Heaven is available* through Jesus Christ himself. This indicates from reading that Jesus died by the cruelty of a dark world; he sacrificed his purity and beauty of mind, body and spirit in the light of reasoning the evils upon the Earth so long ago — and thus brings us back to the responsibility and encouragement of the *Established Church* to light the fire of understanding, compassion, learning, appreciation and the passion of Christ himself, to teach us all the salvation of virtue and knowledge of GOD our father and creator.

To fill seats of salvation is the responsibility of the practices and representatives of the Church and community with inspiration, revelation and consultation.

"But the fruit of the spirit is love, joy, peace, longsuffering, gentleness, goodness, faith, meekness, temperance; against such there is no law. And they that are Christ's have crucified the flesh with the affections and lusts. If we live in the Spirit, let us also walk in the Spirit. Let us not be desirous of vain glory, provoking one another, envying another.

Galatians 5 : 22-26

The modern experiences in life indeed should be truly valued and respected among all men and women for a better world. Our respect and honour should begin at home and our localisation. The history of the world has brought us all once more in dilemma. And from this we must have hope to proceed and understand the word of *God our Father and Creator of virtue, love, honour, respect and truth.*

> *And when you stand praying, forgive, if ye ought against any: that your Father also which is in heaven may forgive you your trespasses. But if you do not forgive, neither will your Father which is in heaven forgive your trespasses.*
>
> *Mark 11 : 25-26*

Chapter Seven

Then cometh Jesus from Galilee to Jordan unto John, to be baptized of him, but John forbad him, saying, I have need to be baptized of thee, and comest thou to me? And Jesus answering said to him, Suffer it to be so now: for thus it becometh us to fulfil all righteousness."

Matthew 3 : 13-15

THE COSMIC ENTRANCEMENT *of us all as humanity* is the unique spectrum of intelligence and our lives upon this planet of life Experiencing Eternity and Evolution. The philanthropic journey of us all with GOD is to Understand Unification and Utilize our science with spiritual resonance. This truth is through a passage with life and experience. As humanity, how do we understand the miracle that we all exist with every day?

GOD our creator is the living proof of everyday existence with Biology, Biogenetics and Belief and the miracle of this message is of Profanity, Proaction and Production of virtuous reasoning! We are a miracle. What do we all know, feel and use our intelligence with this reality for hope and a better future upon this planet of physical limitation and resource?

Our planet is a planet of miracles that happen with every Minute Molecule and Manifestation of Genetics, Gender and Generation. What does this mean for our future? We Grow, Generate and Geometrically use our existence with Knowledge, Knowing and Kinetics with life. So we as humanity are of Sensitivity. Solution and Solace with biological transformation with Biochemistry, Bioengineering and Bodywork. We are a vehicle for science and reasoning, but through manifestations of light protracting and absorbing virtue we walk the Earth with truth.

> *In those days came John the Baptist, preaching in the wilderness of Judea, and saying Repent ye, for the Kingdom of Heaven is at hand. For this is he that was spoken by the Prophet Esaias, saying, "The voice of ONE crying in the wilderness, prepare ye the way of the LORD, make his paths straight.*
>
> ### *Matthew 3 : 1-3*

Humanity is brought today by his intelligence in a modern world of materialism, comforts, and technology. To believe and understand the messages of so long ago we today find this old fashioned. However, the true meaning was a basic foundation of knowledge teaching peoples about our LORD and is profound beauty and honour to all with whom he met. His message was about Humility, Honour and Homage to ordinary people of the World he knew then.

We are all Cosmic Entrancement with GOD. This is a fact, truth and reality and for our future we must all learn to understand this no matter what religion or belief we may have. God is the light of reasoning, salvation and the means of understanding our passage through life. We are all this. The darkness of life is only truly understood when we move forward with reality and reasoning our journey through Cosmic Vibration. We are all part of this structure, evolution and reality both with Heaven and Earth. We are all part of God when we truly open our eyes to truth. We are all part of God through our lessons upon Earth and her biological materialization. We know this as humanity but have forgotten the reality of Cosmic Entrancement through life and journey with time.

Thus we start a new beginning with time and that time is now.

Be at peace with all of life and wonder and the journey we all make through to our destination. For the will of God is at hand without fear, without hate, without desire. We all journey around the Cosmos together aboard this planet of life, biology and tribulation. Our journey is brought together with belief in all things good. Our journey is not forsaken with evil for evil is diminished with love and understanding the Holy works of God and truth. We are all this when we open our eyes and SEE and believe both the here and now and ever more as ONE. We are all this with love, honour and truth.

In the Beginning

AND YASHUA JESUS CHRIST came among the peoples of Israel with messages from God. He taught and healed from his own learning through the Christlight of virtuous reasoning. He GAVE HUMANITY HIS DEVOTION AND LOVE AS ONE. He gave without judgement. He gave without money and influence. He gave to us all his messages of light, love and salvation.

He did not seek fame, fortune or glory. He sought only to bring messages of peace, love, honour and truth to a world in darkness. He was indeed the messiah of all divinity and creed. He was and is the light of the world. His words were the words of God and salvation and light. His presence was the bringer of all Angels of Light and forgiveness. His path was of virtue, honour and love.

Through the stories of the Bible we find him within the scriptures. From ancient until now he was and is a teacher of great knowledge and compassion. Through his life he gave unconditional love to the Earth and humanity. For God so loved the Earth he sent his only son to redeem all men and women, cancelling their sins with understanding and enabling them to overcome the tribulations of life. So through his great person we could find him through two millennia. Our souls undertake life's journey with his love and teaching by our side and a light to shine in the darkness. He gave us all his life and blood through the inhumanity of humanity but his forgiveness was paramount. He did not judge or malign. He gave his love through God our father and creator of all virtue.

So in our prayers we must remember all of our brethren and sisters of life. We share a world of fragmentation but through Yashua Jesus Christ we can find the path of enlightenment and love in a world of great challenge to our virtue. Through his love within eternity we can ever move forward with our lessons in life and the divine love we all seek.

The beauty of life and reasoning is the cosmic entrancement of understanding our validity and truth among our brethren and sisters of life. Healing ourselves brings a light to follow in the footsteps of Yashua Jesus Christ. To understand is to trust, love and honour all things of creation. Despite what we feel with disagreement we are all upon a journey of learning. The answers and questions of life bring us to know the reality of heaven and Earth as one element. To know beauty is to know that all things are for a purpose. That purpose is shown through our choices and decisions of life and journey. Through the beauty of our soul we can indeed find God and his love and wisdom. We can indeed be a person of devotion and creditability to our brethren and sisters of life. Be at one with all things that are pure but understand the pitfalls of decision and choice. The positive elements with Angels and Christ are to know that the universe is the eternal creator of passage with true love and virtue.

Christchurch 2013

Elizabeth Jane Parker

The day began with breakfast and tea
Chatting amiably with cheer and glee
Down to Dorset again with friends
Our journey with time recommends
To walk with wind, rain and snow
Our spirits refined, our faces aglow

With another story to tell so soon
Our journey brings happiness and the room
For each and every holiday we take
Our ears and eyes become awake
The blustering snow gives no respite
Walking to the harbour our souls unite

The welcoming sea, the Fisherman's catch
The scenery unique, so different to match
The winter storms pinching our skin
However it blows, our sight does not dim
The gulls hunch upon the rails
Skimming the sky through snow, they do hail
With loud cries upon the wind
Their survival instincts not to rescind

Seaweed lies upon the shores
Debris from surf and tide restores
The wavering sand builds upon the beach
Causing small dunes within the reach

CHAPTER SEVEN

Of gathering tides that wax and wane
The pattern woven from nature, elegantly remain

Gulls eating the remains of a bird
Nature resolves the hunger reserves
The pattern of life changes each day
The remains will not last, food to repay
The patience of nature seeking to change
The sea and elements to rearrange
We walk with companionship, a route well known
The sands of time have been and shown

A bug hotel for natures' request
The rotting vegetation brings them behest
Of natural sanctuary but a Robin nearby
Picking the bugs for dietary supply
Trees that have fallen are left for infestation
Of natural demise and restoration
For evolution and balance is understood as thus
And from this truth benefits to us

Small gestures from people who care
For natural environment to progressively ensnare
The biological changes that are measured by God
The natural observances
The natural world
The natural messages to us all…

A walk into Christchurch with slippery paths
We waste not the day wrapped with scarfs
The day was icy, wet and cold
But still the scenery a marvel to behold

Visit to the Church a Robin did stray
Friendly, communicative with something to say
That despite the elements of winter today
The beauty of nature is always around
With sight, senses and sound
Within the church there is so much to know
The history, the learning and lessons bestow
Interest, intellect and knowledge to be
From God our Father sanctification is free

The holiday is short but memories live on
The laughter, the fun, the love carries beyond
Each day we're alive we can see so much
The might of God with the gentle touch
The adventures of life is there to endure
Virtue with friendship is always so pure
So love brings us to a place so grand
From our experiences we can all expand
Into the arms of God and truth
Through our lives we need not proof
Of all things good, to remain
With Heaven and Earth
There is always again…
Amen

The Theorem

And he went out from thence, and came into his own country; and his disciples followed him. And when the Sabbath day was come he began to teach in the synagogue; and many hearing him were astonished, saying, from whence hath this man these things? And what wisdom is this given unto him? That even such mighty works are wrought by his hands.

Mark 6 : 1-2

THE EMPHASIS upon our lives as humanity is to understand virtue. The pragmatic positive energies with metaphysics bring us to learn about darkness but also to know the open arena of virtuous reasoning. Negative elements together with self-recognition show the way with forgiveness, honour, respect and devotion to all lateral thinking. We as humanity learn about our world and the downfalls of decision. We learn to overcome all disadvantages with belief in good. We learn that Divine Love is the greatest power of a fragmented world of indecision and dishonour. We learn that the beauty of our soul is an orchestration of melodious composition with God our Father of all.

He without sin cast the first stone upon the muddy waters of time. He without sin knowest small things, for to know God is to know that we are all upon a mission of truth. That truth is about our passage with our Earth and our brethren and sisters as one element of recall with Divine Knowledge. That knowledge combined with virtue is us all vibrationally contained within and without our body of life.

Bless the Lord, O my soul: and all that is within me bless

his holy name.
Bless the Lord O my soul
And forget not his benefits:
Who forgiveth all thine iniquities;
Who healeth all diseases;
Who redeemeth thy life from destruction;
Who crowneth thee with loving kindness and tender mercies:
Who satisfieth thy mouth with good things;
So that thy youth is renewed like an Eagle's
The Lord executeth righteousness;
And judgment for all those oppressed
He made known his ways unto Moses
His acts unto the children of Israel,
The Lord is merciful and gracious.

Psalm 103 : 1-8

Yashua Jesus Christ was our teacher about the ways of salvation. Through him and his tender mercies we are all forgiven. We are all loved and absolved. For the way of life is the miracle of time and reasoning our transgressions. The way of life is about our truth with body and soul as ONE.

My brethren, count it all joy when ye fall into divers' temptations; knowing this that the trying of your faith worketh patience. Let patience do her perfect work, that ye may be perfect and entire, wanting nothing. If any of ye lack wisdom. Let him ask of God, that giveth to men liberally, and upbraideth not; and it shall be given unto him.

CHAPTER SEVEN

James 1 : 2-5

The Lord is our shepherd and he takes us all upon a journey of love and gratitude for all of life and heavenly things. He gave us all his beauty in life and his purpose for us is to know him and be with him forever. We as God's Children learn to love each other despite the World and the darkness now incumbent casting a shadow of doubt among our brethren as to the presence of our Lord. To know as brothers and sisters of life is to follow the way through life understanding the trials and tribulations with Jesus by our side. For his forgiveness and love for us as humanity is a truth we all truly know in our hearts for ever.

Chapter Eight

Intuitive Intuition

With my whole heart I have sought thee
O let me not wander from thy commandments
Thy word I have hid in my heart
That I might not sin against thee
Psalm 119 : 10-11

WE LEARN THE RAMIFICATION *and fealty with Lord Yashua Jesus Christ* through reasoning our virtues with life. We as humanity are upon a quest through the *major domino effect* with life and fellowship. To understand our differences is to know that we are the beneficiaries of God and love. For this has become one of *Universal Opinion* both among followers of Christ and the *Established Church* with consequent fundamentalism and restriction, so to seek and find the foundation stone of our macroscopic vision with God and life we magnify our belief in all things good with hope.

Teach me, O Lord, the way of thy statutes; and I shall keep them to the end.

CHAPTER EIGHT

Psalm 119 : 33

The eternal perpetual motion of time brings the formulation and sermons of God through our belief and transition without reproof from history and the mistakes of the past. We as a Christian move forward with honour and omnivorous passage without omniscient superiority with fellowship. We understand the beauty and love of Christ causing the *Tree of Life* to ramify isotropic substance and respect of all things.

> *Wherewithal shall a young man cleanse his way? By taking heed thereto according to thy word.*
> **Psalm 119.9**

The masquerade of life is about honouring our soul and the light of all things that shine in the darkness. For to understand the purpose of our Lord is to know that he will light our way into a better future and integrity with Earth and her contribution for our lives with God.

> *Moreover brethren, I would not that ye be ignorant, how that all our fathers were under the cloud, and all passed through the sea; were all baptized unto Moses in the cloud and under the sea, and did all eat the same spiritual meat, and did drink the same spiritual drink; for they drank of that spiritual Rock that followed them: and that Rock was Christ.*
>
> **1 Corinthians 10 : 1-4**

To truly understand the Universe with metaphysics is our

mind, body and spirit flowering into the knowledge of the Heavens. God our Father teaches us all to negotiate the pitfalls of life through the divine ordinance and scholastic reasoning of truth and spiritual essence. We as humanity learn to withstand and understand the impermanence of biology and the eternal energies of immanent immeasurable knowledge of time and space, within the spectrum of mindset. The flower of the universe is our intelligence performing the vitalization of wisdom and strength to follow our path through life and reasoning. The cosmetology of the dimensions and ratios of the Universe is circumspect with nihilisms being belief with theism. This is not to contradict thought processes but to learn that all of creation is not based randomly with intelligence but to know that the thesis of scholastics brings us all diverse choice with our one God at the helm. *Determination and Chaos* will philosophically divine physical chemistry with unseen scientific dimensions through space.

> *O God, thou art my God, early will I seek thee: My soul thirsteth for thee, my flesh longeth for thee in a dry and thirsty land where no water is; to SEE thy power and glory, so as I have seen thee in the sanctuary.*

Psalm 63 : 1-2

The effectual transition of life and time gives us energies to live and learn with our soul finding knowledge and love with Earth. The journey we all take is to seek every day our redemption and sanctity with our belief intact. The test of time is the regulator of our individual histories through life seeking with our soul the unification of Heaven and Earth as one element.

A Poem for All Seasons

Elizabeth Jane Parker

A spark of light now *evolved into the night*
The days of love to wonder and ignite
The amour of colour and transition exposed
The undecided disposition disposed
The spring equinox is now formally due
From winter and spring to softly imbue
The answers and questions; formulation and truth
The Seasons of change seeing the proof

Liberation of our soul and Earth to become
The ownership and faculties now as ONE
The Earth is waiting for humanities redemption
The surge of oceans and time to mention
With eternal waves upon the stony shore
Of time unfolding forever more

INTUITIVE INTUITION

The shifting sand, the tides of fate
Walking the shores with time to relate

The gloomy days of winter dissolve
Regulating a new year of resolve
To function with love and attribute and quietude
Within the world of diverse multitude
We walk softly upon the Earth
We walk lovingly towards rebirth
We as humanity must understand
God's unwavering love upon the sand
Of life and meaning of heavenly domain
The gifts of God for all to remain
Within our Hearts we traverse the mountain
With guidance of Angels the eternal fountain
Of love and restoration from above
And the Earth the treasure existing
With time persisting our
Cosmetology viewing the stars
Entering into the theisms at large
With creation and revelation, being our way
With God to teach us in every way
The virtues and pleasure of being in life
Knowing his presence
Knowing his love
Knowing his humanity for us
From above

Seeing an evening Sunset of red and amber
The winding road upon the camber
The colours of a new day
Walking with knowledge upon display
Every day we live a miracle devout

CHAPTER EIGHT

Learning and seeing all about
Our lives with essence and God's elation
For the good revealed within creation
The modern day living, primeval agenda
Living a life with eloquent splendour
For revelation brings the ecstatic vision
With our soul without division
The messages of so long ago to us all
Were with love and quintessence to recall
The Rock of Ages is for us to believe
The beauty and wonder name to relieve
The pressures of darkness that has claimed humanity
Materialism, desire and the vanity
Past times, present and for the future
A life taken for him to forgive
To know the Way
To know the Truth
To know our purpose
To know the knowledge
To know the wonders of the Universe
With the Holy Spirit
Forever

The Revelatory Spin of Sight

THE ASPECTS AND PERSPECTIVE of our sight with God is about the focus of life and reasoning. To pursue our individual story through life is to see the world and her splendour. Walking with God is about learning, seeking and knowing his presence is always around us. Together with our Earth and her resources provided by time is to know that our impermanence as biology will change and diminish with time. But through Yashua Jesus Christ we can believe in and know of his blessings to us all.

> *And surely the mountains falling cometh to nought, and the rock is moved out of his place. The waters wear the stones; thou washest away the things which grow out of the dust of the earth.*
>
> ### *Job 14 : 18-19*

However, our lord does not diminish through time; he waits for us all to follow him with the beauty of our soul and the objectivity of our spirit on earth to recognize the truth of being and humanity. Our belief is eternal when we understand the virtues and love of our God. To see and be with our Lord of gracious mercies is to know of his abiding love despite the cruelty of his passing. We are all the servants of his virtue and love and through him we find our path of determination, understanding our fellowship with compassion and knowledge. Through him we find our true sight in life and reasoning.

> *And behold, two blind men sitting by the wayside, when they heard that Jesus had passed by, cried out, saying, Have mercy on us, O Lord Son of David.*

CHAPTER EIGHT

> *And the Multitude rebuked them, because they should hold their peace: but they cried out the more, Have mercy on us O lord thou son of David. And Jesus stood still, and called them and said, what will ye that I do unto you? They say unto him, Lord that our eyes be opened. So Jesus had compassion on them, and touched their eyes, and immediately their eyes received the sight, and they followed him.*
>
> ### *Matthew 20 : 30-34*

What do we derive from this? His miracles and compassion brought to these men the sight of our Lord and they followed him. Through his blessings and absolve he came unto them, and they sought his beauty and grace by asking for sight. The sight given to the blind revealed the realities and love of God, and we too can ask for sight and follow his way with Truth, honour and absolve. We can learn about his passage through life and his deepening wonder of humanity.

> *For the Law was given by Moses, but grace and truth came by Yashua Jesus Christ. No man has seen God at any time; the only begotten Son, which is in the bosom of the Father, he hath declared him.*
>
> ### *John 1 : 17-18*

The sight of us all is to walk with our soul and see the beauty and truth of life despite the hatred and cruelty ever prevalent today within our world. We as humanity can ever move forward with Jesus and God by our side when we truly understand the way of Love, Honour and truth. We are all part of him who came so many years ago. He gave his life for his knowledge and belief in our one God of all virtues and the eternal beauty of the Universe. He was and is our saviour for all times.

> *...then answered the Jews, and said unto him, what sign showest thou unto us, seeing that thou doest these things" Yashua Jesus answered and said unto them, Destroy this temple, and in three days I will raise it up.*

The First Passover – John 2 : 18-19

But Jesus spoke of his own body, the body of Christ our Savour. And from our lives we all search for rebirth and the lessons of our lives to reach out to Christ. For through him he gives us all the passage we seek from life and suffering back into the realms of virtue and love. We are his temple, and with him as our temple of humanity at the helm, we are all one within the realms of truth and love. And so in as much as our Lord Spake so many years ago, he comes again for our salvation, witnessed by the eyes of all people who truly believe in our Father of Mercies.

> *Peace be to the brethren, and love, with faith, from God our Father and the Lord Yashua Jesus Christ. Grace be with all them that love our Lord Yashua Jesus Christ in sincerity. Amen.*

Ephesians 6 : 23-24

CHAPTER EIGHT

A Bournemouth Story

Elizabeth Jane Parker

Waking with inspiration; *the weekend arrives*
Expectantly optimistic, our new enterprise
Another visit to Bournemouth, a February return
A happy prospect, a winter sojourn
The weather again is grey and dismal so far
But our spirits are not to mar
A prospect of laughter and jolly fun
Our holiday venture has just begun
Although we know; sights are familiar
Each experience is not dissimilar
But the beauty of this place
We know with advantage, knowledge and grace
The beautiful pier visitors will come
Despite the abeyance of morning sun
The yellow sandy beach with curvature and waves
The land and sea the horizon craves
Our eyesight can see panorama and view
Our little adventures we can pursue
The shops, the people the very large balloon
We see again with excitement and soon

INTUITIVE INTUITION

Will walk along the beach today
With diversity, wildlife and people upon display
All free to see with marvel and zest
A life for living with fascination and interest
For variation of circumstance each day will say
A small example of life, of spherical array
The cosmic example of life to explore
The positive construction of finding more
The busy lives we all must lead
Give us respite, a journey relieved
With the sights and sounds we can enjoy
With freedom of spirit our way to employ
Bournemouth an exciting prospect of participation
Into a canvass of rich inspiration
Enjoying the wonders of God and creation
We immerse our self into the congregation
Dogs play happily upon the beach
Throwing the Frisbee so they can reach
Children digging sandcastles with determination
For the reward of building and inspiration
Buckets and spades, joggers go by
The diachronic aspirations do fly
Upon the winding path of living
The miracle, the time is now forgiving
With God we find our adventure is free
Without the money we can all see
The wonder of seeing upon our sphere
The joys of God that we are here
Today with laughter
With fun
With elevation
With love

CHAPTER EIGHT

The Sun descends across the water with silver and gold
Clouds weaving their way and unfold
With light shimmering and reflecting upon the sea
The beauty is there for everyone to see
A photographer takes this wondrous pose
Of natural beauty to expose
Not diminishing with fascination we stare
A miraculous display while standing there
The cosmic entrancement of colours and light
Skimming and shimmering for our sight
The water loses the grey and dour
Instead the mirror image and power
The wonder, the impact of God
The imagination of God
The blessings of God
The inspiration of God
There to see and enjoy
Is free
For us all wherever we may be
His love is great
His love forever
His love for us

Chapter Nine

Fortitude and Ambivalences

To Walk with Jesus is to know that long ago he came to teach us about God, virtue, truth and love. We as humanity overlook this today with modernism and materialism. Thus to seek with the knowledge of Jesus is to know that he brought us all the love of Heaven and the Way of life with Earth understanding all perspectives with God.

THE WORLD IN WHICH WE LIVE *both spiritually and biologically* is the valuation of our soul-seeking with life and reason. The contradictions through our journey may seem at odds, and the aberration of timescale at whatever period of life will always change with demonstrable metaphysics with biological transition.

Our learning through life may realistically appear as a paradox with our steadfast belief in an unseen phenomenon and relationship with God. The ups and downs of our learning can become painful and laborious. The way forward may seem daunting one day and wonderful the next. So to merit our soul and proceed with virtue, we acknowledge the difficulties we may face. The challenges of life for our Billions of humanity are upon a Planet of Life and sustenance is multifarious with insurmountable pressure upon both man's intelligence and his desires. How do we actually know and trust the love and measurability of the Universe and the power of God?

The solace to us all is thus:

> *Be ye therefore followers of God, as dear children: and walk in love, as Christ has also loved us, and has given himself for offering and a sacrifice to God for a sweet-smelling savour.*
>
> ***Ephesians 5 : 1-2***

> *For ye were sometimes in darkness, but now are ye light in the Lord: walk as children of light; (for the fruit of the Spirit is in all goodness and righteousness and truth ;) proving what is acceptable unto the Lord. And have no fellowship with the unfruitful works of darkness, but rather reprove them.*
>
> ***Ephesians 5 : 8-11***

> *SEE then that ye walk circumspectly, not as fools, but as wise, redeeming the time, because the days of evil. Wherefore ye be not unwise, but understanding what the WILL of the Lord is.*
>
> ***Ephesians 5 : 15-17***

From our lessons through life we as individuals have many and diversify with our numbers. However, to seek and find our *Lord of Mercies* is to know that he does not judge, but meets us as individuals. Finding our Lord is about the virtues of life, knowledge, love and compassion towards our fellowship. These are often tested with modern-day media and sensationalism. However, to know Jesus is to know that he loves us unconditionally and to seek his forgiveness is about forgiving ourselves and others first. He gave his life to show us his forgiveness as a man who suffered for his truth and belief with God and the wonders of the Universe beyond our sight in life. He gave us his virtue above all men and their sins. He gave us his knowledge and fortitude through millennia of Roman Dictatorship and influence. He gave us his time and his valuation of honour and love. So in our modern world we can all find him through his compassion, love and truth for the knowledge and blessings of Heaven above and the Earth and her beauty for our salvation.

> *Peace be to the brethren, and love with faith, from God the Father and the Lord Jesus Christ. Grace be with all them that love our Lord Jesus Christ in sincerity. Amen.*

> ***Ephesians 6 : 23-24***

CHAPTER NINE

The Divine Providence

HUMANITY IN A MODERN WORLD is very much divided in belief and a future towards betterment in the brethren of life and reasoning. Jesus Christ emerged in an age where mankind was depleting his knowledge and love of life and reasoning. Dictatorial aspects of supreme incomprehension about humility, honour, compassion evolved with mankind and the leaders of those times. Thus again, we find ourselves unable to know with whom knowledge, honour, truth and compassion is found. Our belief as human beings is distorted without respect and honour towards life and reasoning within a planet of limitations and resources. Do we really want to know this as a truth as well as fact?

We ask within these dark times, who really understands the way of life and reasoning? We live with bio-diversity and growth with nature. From nature come our resources to live within a world of limitations. We know this and are taught about the energies with a Planet of evolution and time with space. Within our modern world we have acknowledged carbon prints and the ozone layer. We know that our world evolved from fragility and balance. We know this, we are taught this. However, our intelligence with life does not listen to the warnings given. We have limitations of lifespan, ecology, bio-diversity and transition through time. We know this. However, how do we respect this and acknowledge this today with our intelligences throughout our world of limitation?

Jesus Christ came to us through dark millennia of dictatorships and influence. He came to tell us about God and the truth. He came to explain about our journey through life and the reasoning of our soul to seek, learn and grow with time and space. He came to explain his love for us and our errors. He came with his followers to bring messages of wisdom and philanthropic love of all things relating to God's creation. His humility and bearing brought the light of Christian love and honour to all, and to know the laws of God and the divine right of humanity to live and learn with virtue. Yes, virtue is a word to explain about God our Father to whom we all belong. But as his children we have not heard him today within this modern world of dilemma. And thus we must speak the truth and as said, "United we stand, divided we fall." What does this mean? We all have choices in life and despite the hatred that exists among our brethren throughout the world we have yet to listen to a man who gave his life for us to know and believe in the power of love and God our Father. To find this man we all need to listen to his wisdom and devotion for our betterment—so we can move forward with the positive elements of electro-dynamism with time, learning and proactive mind-sets.

We do not discriminate against other beliefs, but delight in the knowledge that to know that a man devoted to us all gave his life to demonstrate the love of God to a world in downfall. His meaning was about brotherhood and sisterhood, understanding the beauty of life and reasoning to know that we are loved in another dimension of purity and peace. We are loved and forgiven our trespasses. Not so today in a world caught in debt, desire and need throughout the world. From this we start to lose our inheritance, and that inheritance consists of the values of our Earth and her gifts to us all in a world in which we live.

The soul of Jesus is thus expressed in the words of the psalmist:

> *Commit thy way unto the Lord; trust also in him; and he shall bring it to pass. And he shall bring forth thy righteousness as the light, and thy judgement as the noonday. Rest in the Lord, and wait patiently for him…*

Psalm 37 : 5-7

Afterword

One God One Truth One Love

"The Natural Law of the Universe is based upon spherical rotation. Through the annals of multiplex intelligence and logic we as mankind have been taught to understand science and truth. The factual elements of transitions evolve through sacred and ancient memory through DNA and life with God our creator and his messengers of virtue. To follow our lives with vision is to know theism as one of good no matter what creed or religion and God our Father shows us all his love when we truly believe and learn through life's journey."

Elizabeth Jane Parker, May 2013

THE EMPHASIS OF IDEOLOGY within Divine Science is to know that Determination is to substantiate order out of the Chaos Theory of revelations and substance with status. The Universe is us all through life and reasoning and the Cosmic Entrancement of spiritual attainment with virtue is the success of our subconscious learning and our creative autonomy with bodily learning. To bring Jesus Christ into catabolism and energies with Earth and her Dynamics is to realise that we are not alone through our journey with life. For our Earth is the foundation of our lives and the experiences we have each day of living.

The Molecules of our existence collaborate with our mindset and journey and to understand the Christlight of existence is to realise that creation came from God. How do we know? Science has many theories to this. And so we search for answers and these answers allow our Universal Intelligence to question and learn about the dynamics of history, geography, religion, politics, biochemistry and all aspects of our lives upon Earth.

So we ask about Jesus Christ and his knowledge and teachings during his life as a great teacher. His University and Ministry was one of Judaism and Holy Scripture with Angels. However, modern-day living and science has become one of nihilism and social nonentity with God. The fragmentation of many societies hangs in the balance between desire and materialism. The simple truth is we as humanity as brothers and sisters have lost our way upon a beautiful planet of life. Who cares? Who wonders? Who knows?

We are impermanent and our lives change physically and emotionally. We all find reasons not to believe in the creative circumstances of daily life and the sustainability aspect of journey during 2013 and are now confronting an unsubstantiated dilemma throughout our world. If this diagnosis appears somewhat morose, the human aspect of us all is being lost within a jungle of desire and technological dynamics. To understand the percentage of our brain power is to know that we all discharge individualistic tendencies for our own ends and not the teachings of a man who came so many years ago to teach about our truth and the God of love.

We are all brothers and sisters of life and reasoning. We all have the capability to transcend into the realms of joy, understanding the wonders of life and our journey. We all have the ability to share and create a better world for us all. This comes with the light of sharing and caring for each other and securing our identities as one without the need and greed of a modern world.

To make sense of God is to listen and observe the natural world from whence we all came and know that he takes joy in the balance and beauty of nature. We all have the ability to take time out and study and learn about the Natural World and wonder at the amazing natural transformations that occur every day within our world.

> *And he spake unto them a parable; Behold the Fig Tree, and all the trees; when they now shoot forth, you see and know of your own selves that summer is nigh at hand. So likewise ye, when ye see these things come to pass, ye know that the Kingdom of God is at hand. Verily I say unto to you, this generation shall not pass away, till all is fulfilled.*
>
> ### *Luke 21 : 29-32*

To make sense of our lives is to know that our adjudication and transcendence with virtue appeases all downfalls when we understand the truth and power of Angelic Kinetics. Their attraction is not about speciality for ego and people who seek in our modern world, to use and abuse the Systems of Analysis from Universal Strategy; the true love of God is about us all and individualism will not ascend into the domains of truth and understanding with ego. Desire for glory and fame are not conducive with Divine Reasoning and Science. However, this is not bringing fear but to learn about the Wonders of Life and God within the spherical realisation about evolution and change. The retrograde aspect of planetary alignment is about the manoeuvrability of our soul and spirit together. Then pragmatics and assimilation with Cosmic Entrancement means the realisation of our wishing to follow Jesus Christ in the forever terminology of the Holy Trinity and the true God of love in fellowship.

Our lives and reasoning are the virtuous ways of understanding evolution, nature and the changes of our ever-moving planet around the Sun. Our reasoning should be maintained and contained along the road of love, honour and truth.

> *Therefore do my thoughts cause me to answer, and for this I make haste. I have heard the check of my reproach, and the spirit of my understanding causest me to answer. Knoweth thou not this of old, since man was placed upon Earth...?*
>
> **Job 20 : 2-4**

And so the Lord is my Shepherd and I shall not want or need desire. Upon the road upon salvation we all share and care for each other and thus humanity will once more find the truth of God and reasoning.

The Beginning

The Cosmic Entrancement & the Big SEE

THE PARALLAX THINKING OF MODERN SOCIETY is to believe that all aspects of faith are predominately male with the dominance of the patriarchal aspect and perception within the spectrum of learning with its male orientation. The intellectual forum within our world is comparable with sanguine belief in all things good. So the reasoning of men throughout recorded history indicates that women have secondary meaning in life. This truth is apparent within the Holy Bible of medieval and former writings. The modern Church embraces women within the congregation but disallows without flexibility the importance of their role within Society. And yet, discreetly within the Holy Bible, wisdom is a woman. But still women are disallowed a Bishopric with the Established Church during 2013.

The simplicity of life without the female species is obvious; we would not exist and all aspects of humanity would not be known. This is a truth and yet worldwide at present women are still considered non-essential when representing God our Father. Our sisters of life are overlooked within the annuals of time and space with life. So all aspects of truth analogy is to believe both in man and woman as holy entities of Christ and know that the love of God is the maintenance of this truth. We all journey together upon this Planet of Life. Man or Woman, we all have a purpose. Man and woman, we all belong to the human race and the God-given intelligence of both procreation and creative energies of love and truth. We all learn, live and understand. We are all brothers and sisters of light, life and leniency, both to ourselves and each other.

The vision of us all begins with a big SEE (the Spiritual Evolution Event); this beginning brings equality to the forum and evangelical aspect of faith.

It has been recorded that Mary Magdalene saw Jesus as the Holy Spirit after his crucifixion and through her sight and connection he was known throughout the World of Christianity. The simplicity of this was hidden by history and tyranny. The world of men disguised her true meaning with Christianity and the Jewish denomination with God's word. Modern-day intellectuals recognise this and through a televised medium portrayed her importance in the history of Jewish/Christian belief; history has hidden her role within the Established Church. But all leanings and learning bring us to know that Women hold within their hearts the same reasons and trust of God our Father. The changes must be known throughout the world and the importance of World peace and love among our brethren and sisters together — to bring a future of hope, love and transition to a World currently in dilemma and without purpose as humanity and as ONE. The intellectual emphasis with reasoning is that we all share a world of wonder and habitation. This world Earth brings life to us all as humanistic equals. The denial aspect brings strong opinion and denial within the forum of communication and lecture to those people who find "the white light" a difficulty to understand. For God is the white light of reasoning to us through life and learning agenda and we all have the ability to seek and find our virtue within the spectrum of this miracle. And despite the evil that continues throughout the globe we can all find our salvation, learning and absolving the many issues prevalent within Societies today.

If God seems to be a lecture, then we must understand that denial is a powerful delusion and the reality we all should live upon Earth; we fail to SEE the beauty of life and journey. God is the science and reasoning of us all despite disbelief and the workings of materialism during our modern societies and thus from this, we live and learn to SEE our world with fact and truth forming a better world. We learn to negotiate all downfalls and upturns with proaction without reaction. We learn to use the wisdom of our Masters within the realms of the White Light. We learn that God is us as eternity and the beauty upon Earth and within Heaven.

God bless and eternal love

Elizabeth Jane Parker